Impressum
Verlag: BABADADA GmbH, Nedderfeld 112 , 22529 Hamburg
Geschäftsführer / Verlagsleitung: Harald Hof
Druck: Books on Demand GmbH, In de Tarpen 42, 22848 Norderstedt

Imprint
Publisher: BABADADA GmbH, Nedderfeld 112 , 22529 Hamburg, Germany
Managing Director / Publishing direction: Harald Hof
Print: Books on Demand GmbH, In de Tarpen 42, 22848 Norderstedt

學校
school

除
divide

186/2

黑板
board

教室
classroom

校園
school yard

老師
teacher

紙
paper

筆
pen

辦公桌
desk

直尺
ruler

書
book

書寫
write

學生
pupil

書包
satchel

鉛筆盒
pencil case

鉛筆
pencil

削鉛筆機
pencil sharpener

橡皮擦
rubber

畫板
drawing pad

圖畫
drawing

畫筆
paintbrush

顏料盒
paint box

剪刀
scissors

膠水
glue

練習冊
exercise book

家庭作業
homework

12

數字
number

2+2

加
add

5-2

減
subtract

2×2

乘
multiply

計算
calculate

A

字母
letter

ABCDEFG
HIJKLMN
OPQRSTU
VWXYZ

字母表
alphabet

hello

字
word

課文

text

讀

read

粉筆

chalk

上課

lesson

登記

register

考試

examination

證書

certificate

校服

school uniform

教育

education

百科全書

encyclopedia

大學

university

顯微鏡

microscope

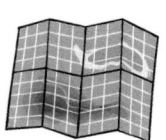

地圖

map

廢紙簍

waste-paper basket

旅行

travel

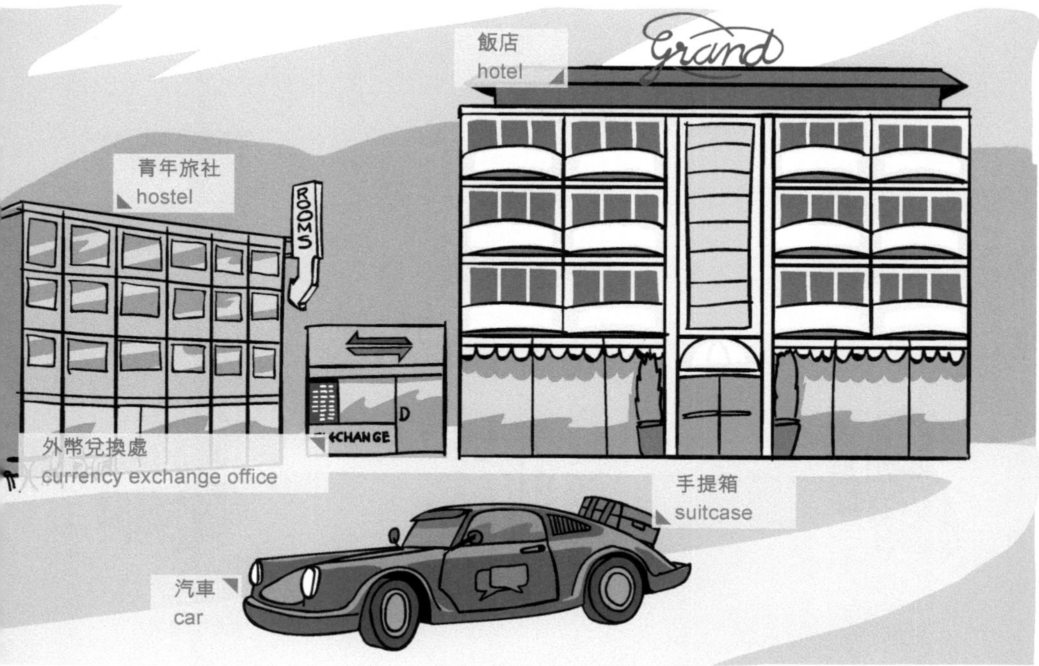

飯店
hotel
Grand
青年旅社
hostel
ROOMS
外幣兌換處
currency exchange office
手提箱
suitcase
汽車
car

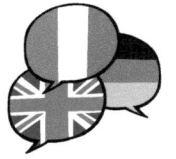

語言

language

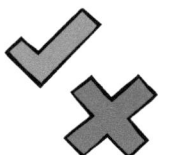

是/否

yes / no

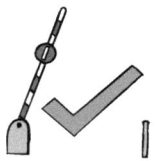

好的

Okay

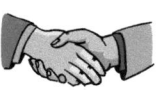

您好

hello

翻譯人員

translator

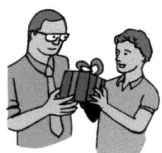

謝謝

Thank you

……多少錢？

how much is…?

我不明白

I don´t get it

問題

problem

晚上好！

Good evening!

早上好！

Good morning!

晚安！

Good night!

再見

goodbye

方向

direction

行李

luggage

包

bag

背包

backpack

客人

guest

房間

room

睡袋

sleeping bag

帳篷

tent

旅行資訊

tourist information

海灘

beach

信用卡

credit card

早餐

breakfast

午餐

lunch

晚餐

dinner

票

Ticket

電梯

elevator

郵票

stamp

邊界

border

海關

customs

大使館

embassy

簽證

visa

護照

passport

交通運送

transport

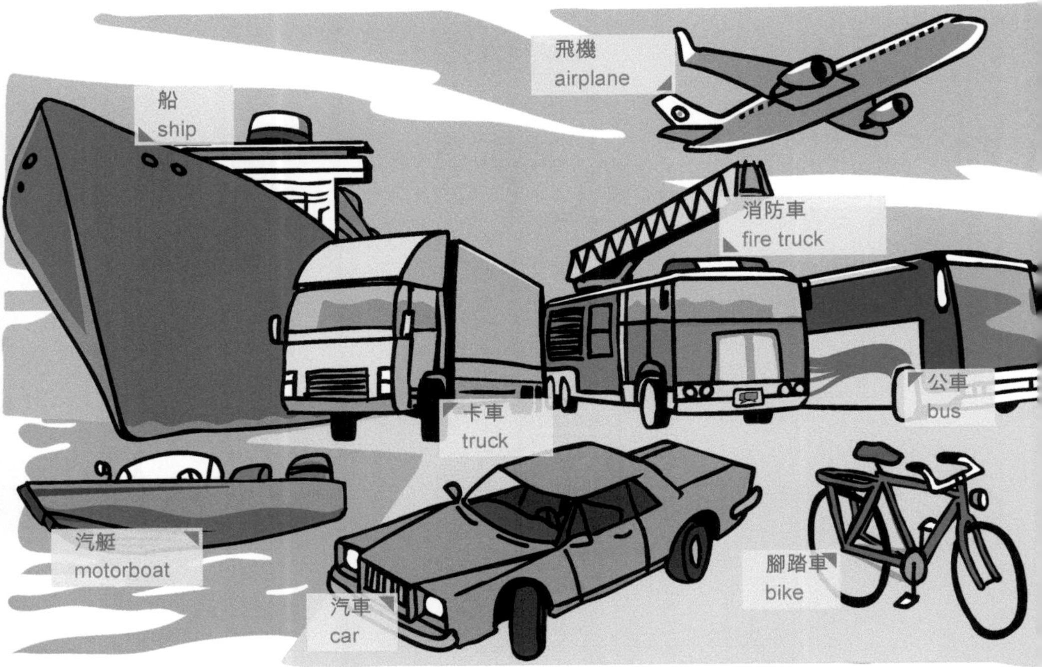

飛機
airplane
船
ship
消防車
fire truck
公車
bus
卡車
truck
汽艇
motorboat
汽車
car
腳踏車
bike

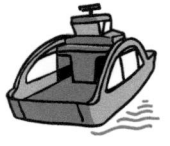

渡輪

ferry

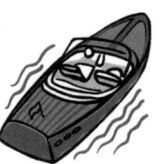

小船

boat

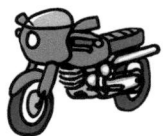

機車

motorbike

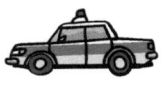

警車

police car

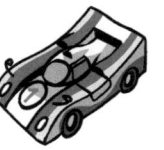

賽車

racing car

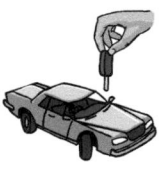

租車

rental car

拼車
car sharing

拖車
tow truck

垃圾車
garbage truck

馬達
engine

汽油
fuel

加油站
fuel station

交通標識
traffic sign

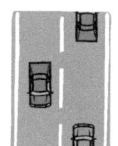

交通
traffic

交通堵塞
traffic jam

停車場
parking lot

火車站
train station

軌道
tracks

火車
train

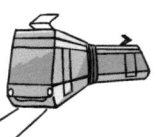

路面電車
tram

客車廂
wagon

直升機

helicopter

機場

airport

塔

tower

乘客

passenger

集裝箱

container

紙板箱

carton

手推車

cart

籃子

basket

起飛/降落

take off / land

城市
city

村莊

village

市中心

city center

房子

house

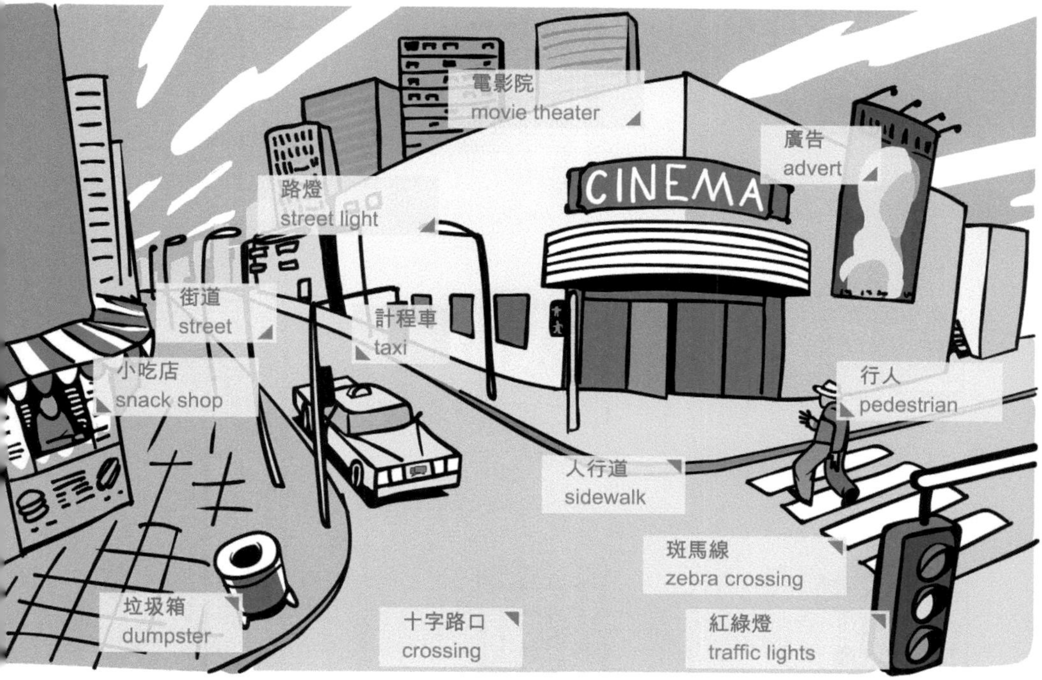

電影院
movie theater
CINEMA
廣告
advert
路燈
street light
街道
street
計程車
taxi
小吃店
snack shop
行人
pedestrian
人行道
sidewalk
斑馬線
zebra crossing
垃圾箱
dumpster
十字路口
crossing
紅綠燈
traffic lights

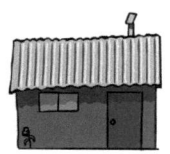

小屋

hut

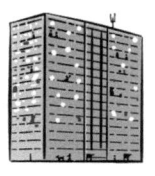

公寓

apartment

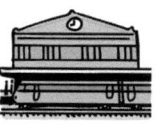

火車站

train station

市政廳

city hall

MUSEUM

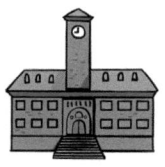

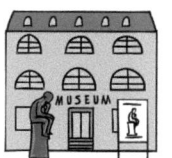

博物館

museum

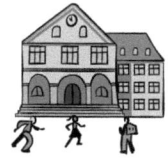

學校

school

大學
university

銀行
bank

醫院
hospital

飯店
hotel

藥房
pharmacy

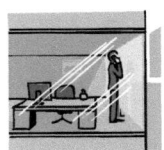

辦公室
office

書店
book shop

商店
shop

花店
flower shop

超市
supermarket

市場
market

百貨商店
department store

魚店
fishmonger's shop

購物中心
mall

海港
harbor

公園
park

長凳
bench

橋
bridge

樓梯
stairs

捷運
subway

隧道
tunnel

公車站
bus stop

酒吧
bar

餐館
restaurant

郵筒
postbox

路標
street sign

停車計時器
parking meter

動物園
zoo

游泳池
swimming pool

清真寺
mosque

農場
farm

污染
pollution

墓地
cemetery

教堂
church

操場
playground

寺廟
temple

地形
landscape

樹葉
leaf

指示牌
signpost

路
path

草地
meadow

石頭
stone

樹
tree

徒步旅行者
hiker

河
river

草
grass

花
flower

峽谷

valley

丘陵

hill

湖

lake

森林

forest

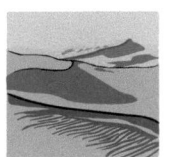

沙漠

desert

火山

volcano

城堡

castle

彩虹

rainbow

蘑菇

mushroom

棕櫚樹

palm tree

蚊子

mosquito

蒼蠅

fly

螞蟻

ant

蜜蜂

bee

蜘蛛

spider

地形 - landscape

甲蟲
beetle

青蛙
frog

松鼠
squirrel

刺蝟
hedgehog

野兔
hare

貓頭鷹
owl

鳥
bird

天鵝
swan

野豬
boar

鹿
deer

麋鹿
moose

水壩
dam

風力發電機
wind turbine

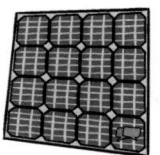

太陽能電池板
solar panel

氣候
climate

餐館
restaurant

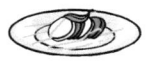

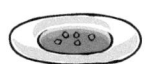

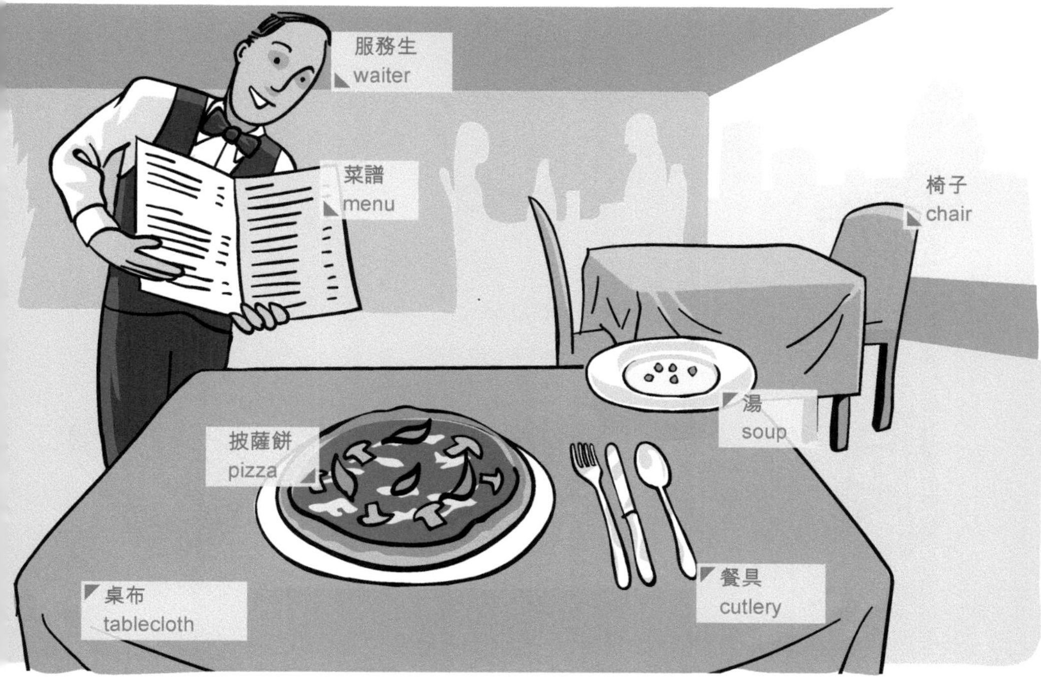
服務生
waiter
菜譜
menu
椅子
chair
湯
soup
披薩餅
pizza
桌布
tablecloth
餐具
cutlery

前菜

starter

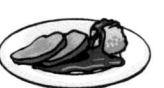

主菜

main course

甜點

dessert

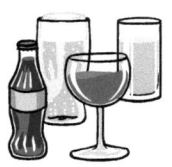

飲料

drinks

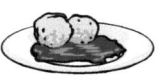

食物

food

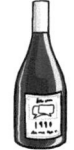

瓶子

bottle

速食

fast food

街邊小吃

street food

茶壺

teapot

糖盒

sugar bowl

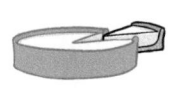

一份飯菜

portion

義式咖啡機

espresso machine

高腳椅

high chair

帳單

bill

托盤

tray

刀

knife

餐叉

fork

勺子

spoon

茶匙

teaspoon

餐巾

serviette

玻璃杯

glass

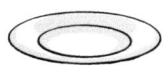

碟子
plate

湯盤
soup plate

碟子
saucer

醬
sauce

鹽瓶
salt shaker

胡椒研磨罐
pepper mill

醋
vinegar

食用油
oil

調味料
spices

番茄醬
ketchup

芥末
mustard

美乃滋
mayonnaise

超市

supermarket

特價
special offer
FOR
顧客
customer
乳製品
dairy products
水果
fruit
購物車
shopping cart

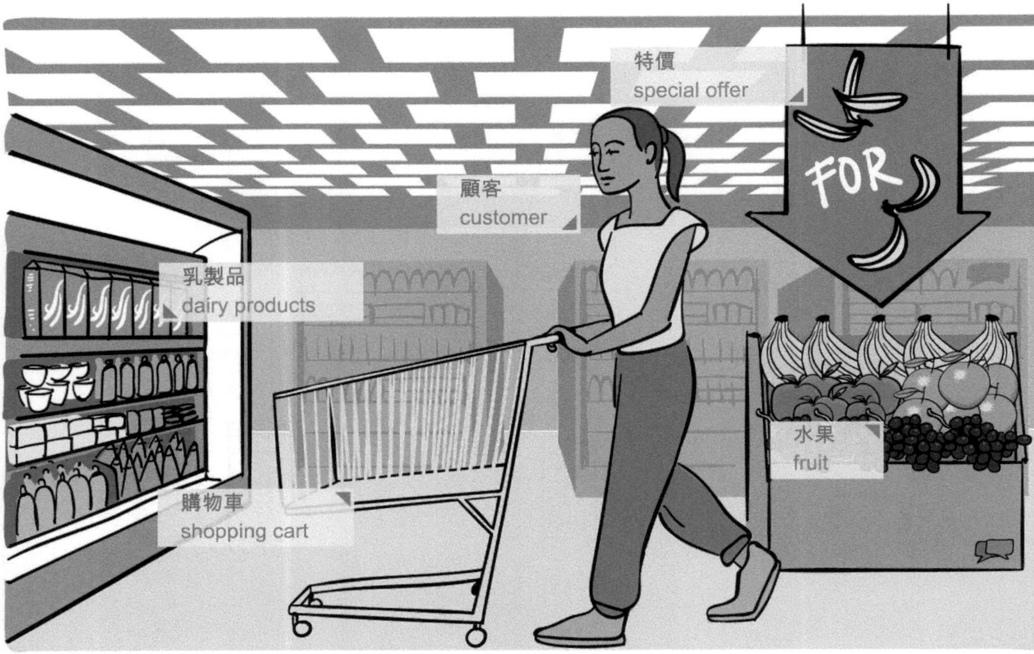

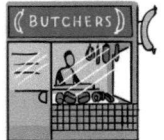

BUTCHERS

肉鋪

butcher's shop

BAKERY

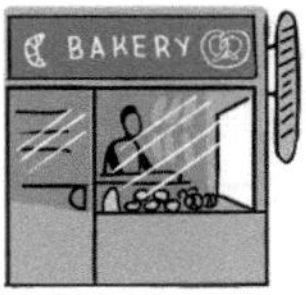

麵包店

bakery

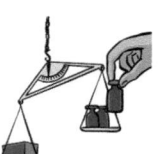

稱重

weigh

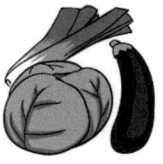

蔬菜

vegetables

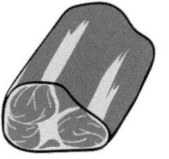

肉

meat

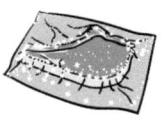

冷凍食品

frozen food

冷盤
cold cuts

罐頭食品
canned food

洗衣粉
detergent

甜食
candy

日用品
household products

清潔用品
cleaning products

銷售員
sales representative

收銀機
cash register

收銀員
cashier

購物清單
shopping list

開放時間
opening hours

錢包
wallet

信用卡
credit card

袋子
bag

塑膠袋
plastic bag

水

water

果汁

juice

牛奶

milk

可樂

coke

紅酒

wine

啤酒

beer

酒

alcohol

可可

cocoa

茶

tea

咖啡

coffee

義式濃縮咖啡

espresso

卡布奇諾

cappuccino

香蕉

banana

蘋果

apple

柳丁

orange

西瓜

melon

檸檬

lemon

胡蘿蔔

carrot

大蒜

garlic

竹子

bamboo

洋蔥

onion

蘑菇

mushroom

堅果

nuts

麵條

noodles

義大利麵

spaghetti

米飯

rice

沙拉

salad

薯條

fries

炸馬鈴薯

fried potatoes

披薩餅

pizza

漢堡

hamburger

三明治

sandwich

炸豬排

escalope

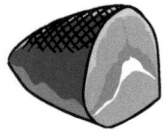

火腿

ham

義大利臘腸

salami

香腸

sausage

雞肉

chicken

烤肉

roast

魚

fish

燕麥片
porridge oats

木斯里
muesli

玉米片
cornflakes

麵粉
flour

牛角麵包
croissant

麵包捲
bread roll

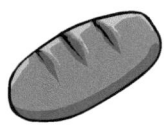

麵包
bread

吐司
toast

餅乾
cookies

奶油
butter

凝乳
curd

蛋糕
cake

蛋
egg

煎蛋
fried egg

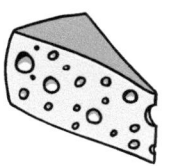

起司
cheese

食物 - food

冰淇淋

ice cream

糖

sugar

蜂蜜

honey

果醬

jelly

巧克力醬

nougat cream

咖哩

curry

農場

farm

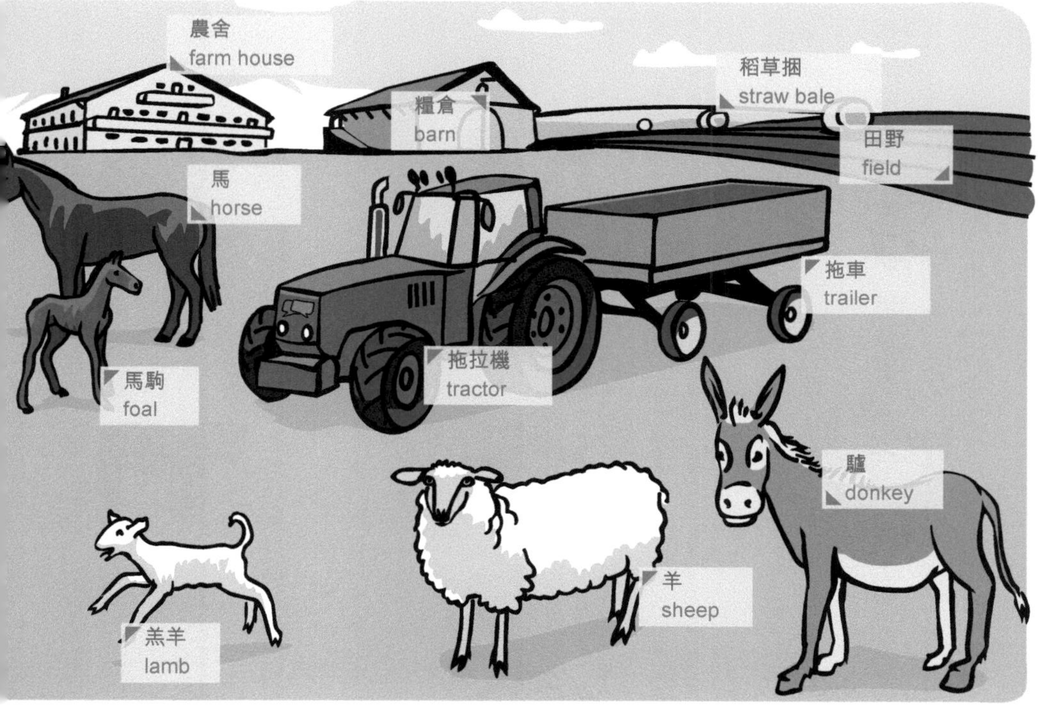
農舍
farm house
稻草捆
straw bale
糧倉
barn
田野
field
馬
horse
拖車
trailer
拖拉機
tractor
馬駒
foal
驢
donkey
羊
sheep
羔羊
lamb

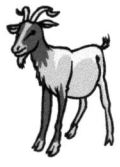

山羊

goat

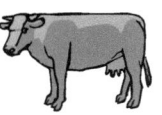

奶牛

cow

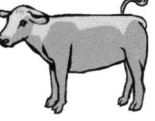

小牛

calf

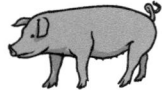

豬

pig

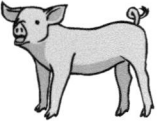

小豬

piglet

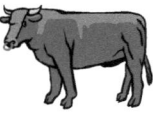

公牛

bull

鵝

goose

鴨

duck

小雞

chick

母雞

hen

公雞

cockerel

鼠

rat

貓

cat

老鼠

mouse

牛

ox

狗

dog

狗屋

dog house

花園澆水軟管

garden hose

澆水壺

watering can

長柄大鐮刀

scythe

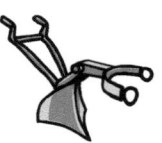

犁

plow

鐮刀
sickle

鋤頭
hoe

長柄草耙
pitchfork

斧頭
axe

獨輪手推車
pushcart

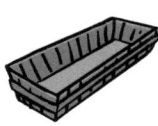

飼料槽
trough

牛奶罐
milk can

麻布袋
sack

柵欄
fence

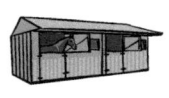

馬廄
stable

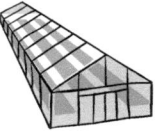

溫室
greenhouse

土壤
soil

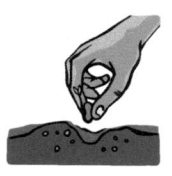

種子
seed

肥料
fertilizer

聯合收割機
combine harvester

收割

harvest

收割

harvest

地瓜

yams

小麥

wheat

大豆

soya

土豆

potato

玉米

corn

油菜籽

rapeseed

果樹

fruit tree

樹薯

manioc

穀物

grain

房子
house

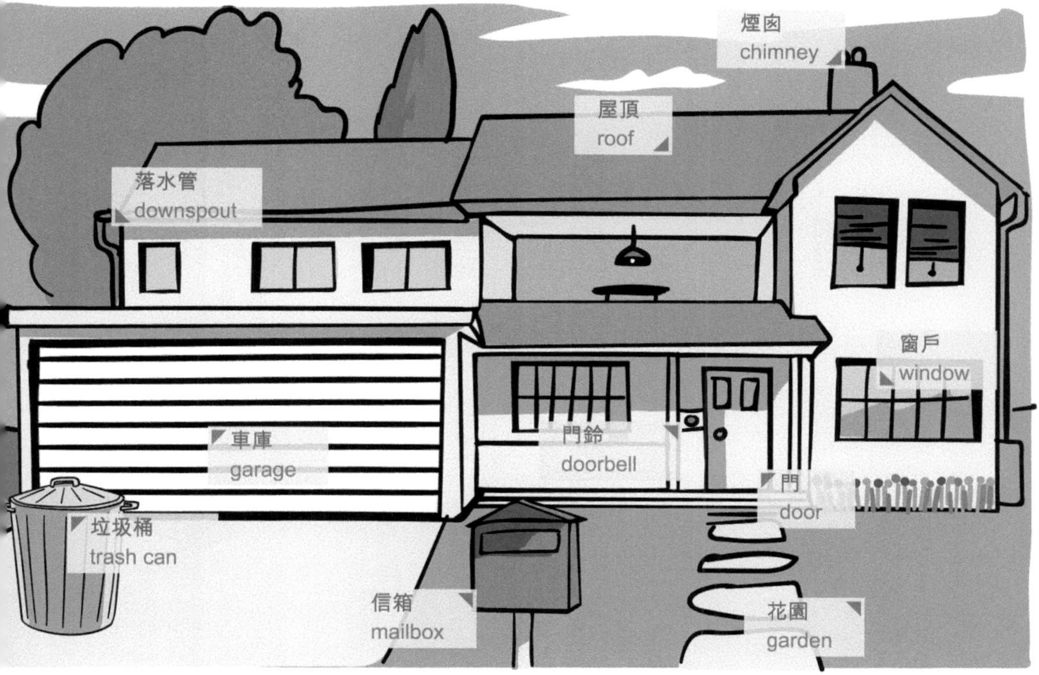

煙囪
chimney

屋頂
roof

落水管
downspout

窗戶
window

車庫
garage

門鈴
doorbell

門
door

垃圾桶
trash can

信箱
mailbox

花園
garden

客廳
living room

浴室
bathroom

廚房
kitchen

臥室
bedroom

兒童房
kids room

餐廳
dining room

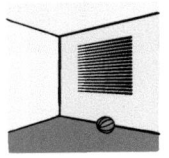

地板
floor

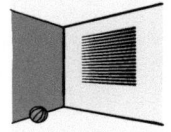

牆壁
wall

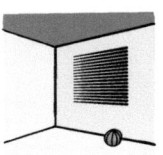

天花板
ceiling

地窖
cellar

三溫暖
sauna

陽臺
balcony

露臺
terrace

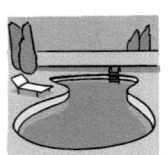

游泳池
pool

割草機
lawn mower

被單
sheet

床罩
bedspread

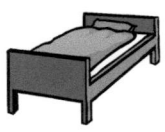

床
bed

掃帚
broom

水桶
bucket

開關
switch

房子 - house

客廳

living room

壁紙
wallpaper
相片
picture
檯燈
lamp
擱架
shelf
櫥櫃
cabinet
電視
television
壁爐
fireplace
花
flower
墊子
cushion
沙發
sofa
花瓶
vase
遙控器
remote control

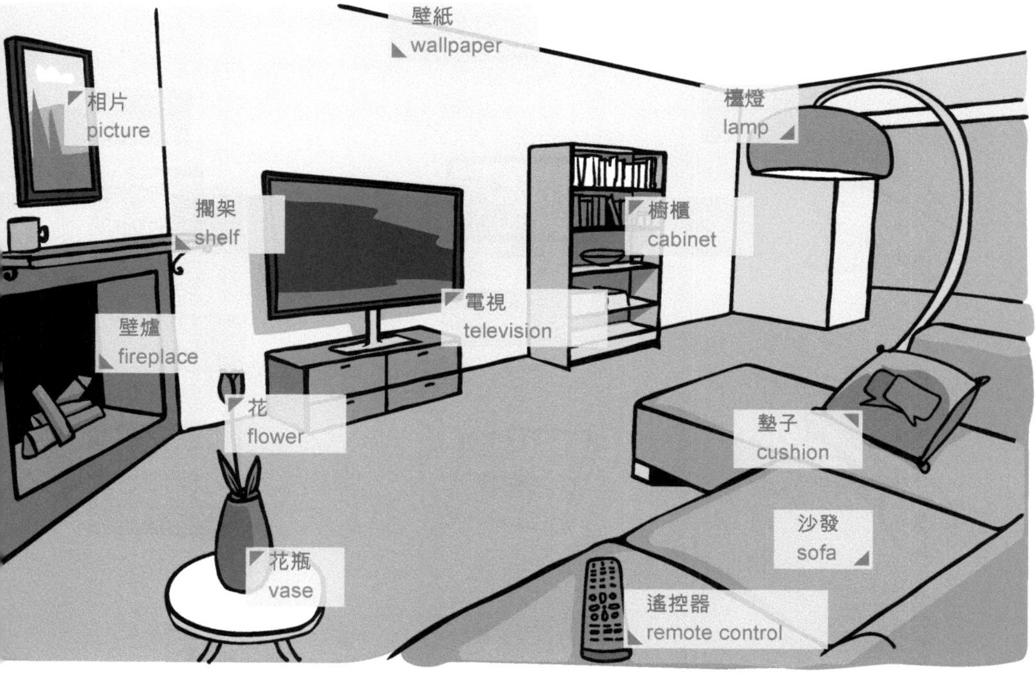

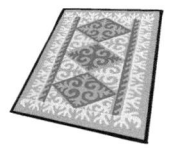

地毯

carpet

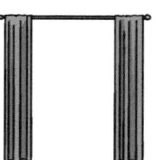

窗簾

drape

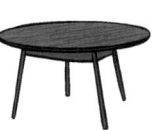

餐桌

table

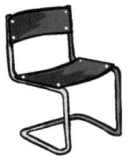

椅子

chair

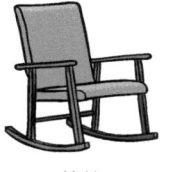

搖椅

rocking chair

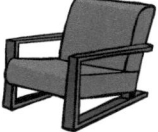

扶手椅

armchair

書
book

毯子
blanket

裝飾品
decoration

木柴
firewood

電影
film

高傳真音響
stereo system

鑰匙
key

報紙
newspaper

油畫
painting

海報
poster

收音機
radio

筆記本
notebook

吸塵器
vacuum cleaner

仙人掌
cactus

蠟燭
candle

廚房

kitchen

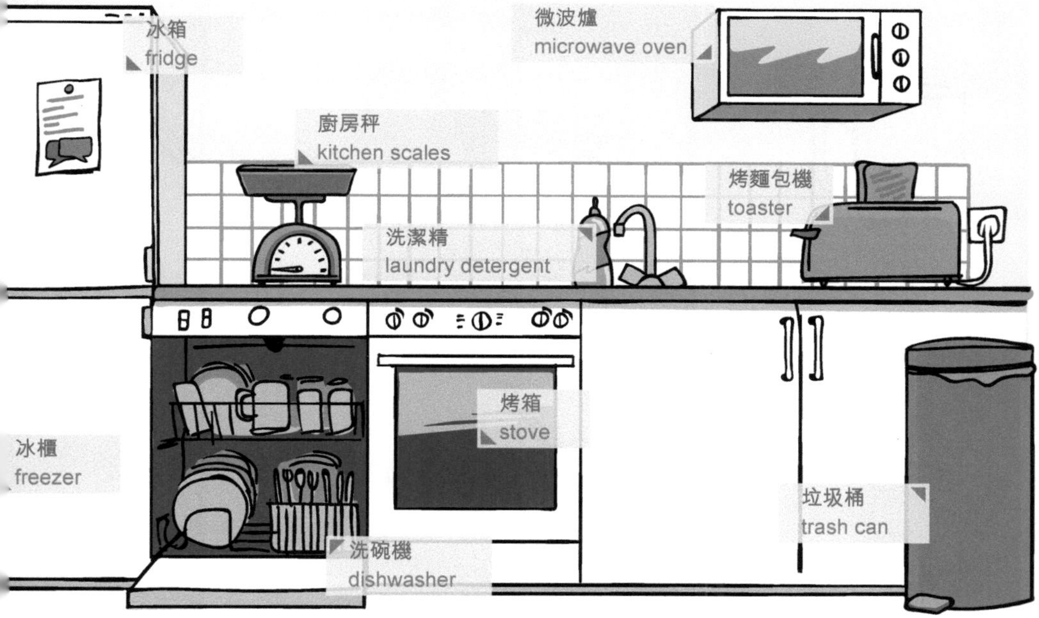

冰箱
fridge
微波爐
microwave oven
廚房秤
kitchen scales
烤麵包機
toaster
洗潔精
laundry detergent
烤箱
stove
冰櫃
freezer
垃圾桶
trash can
洗碗機
dishwasher

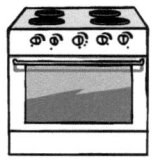

炊具

cooker

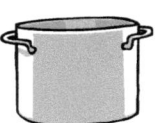

鍋

pot

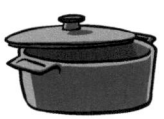

鑄鐵鍋

cast-iron pot

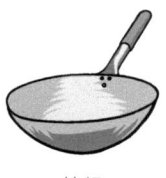

炒鍋

wok / kadai

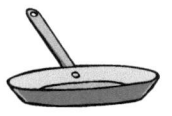

平底鍋

pan

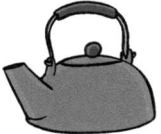

水壺

kettle

蒸鍋

steamer

烤盤

baking tray

陶瓷鍋

crockery

馬克杯

mug

碗

bowl

筷子

chopsticks

長柄勺

ladle

鏟子

spatula

攪拌器

whisk

濾網

strainer

篩子

sieve

磨碎機

grater

研缽

mortar

燒烤

barbecue

明火

fireplace

菜板
chopping board

擀麵杖
rolling pin

開瓶器
corkscrew

罐子
can

開罐器
can opener

隔熱手套
oven cloth

水槽
sink

刷子
brush

海綿
sponge

攪拌機
blender

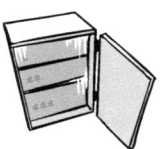

冷藏箱
deep freezer

奶瓶
baby bottle

水龍頭
tap

浴室

bathroom

淋浴
shower
供暖裝置
heating
毛巾
towel
浴簾
shower curtain
泡沫浴
bubble bath
浴缸
bathtub
玻璃杯
glass
洗衣機
washing machine
水龍頭
tap
瓷磚
tiles
便壺
potty
水槽
sink

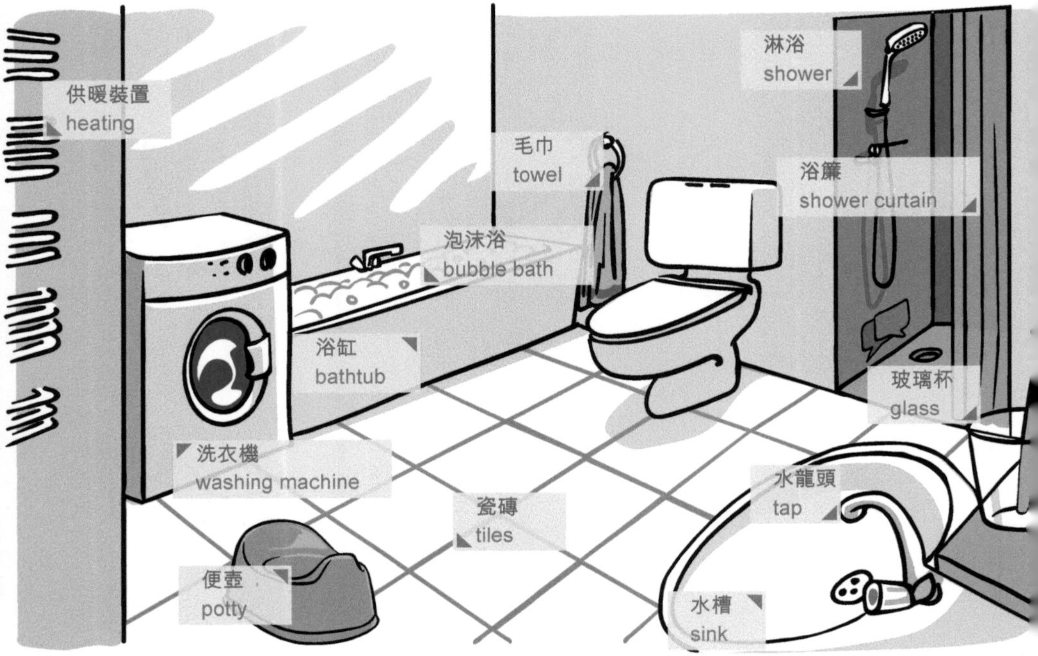

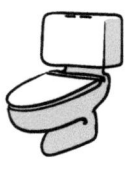

廁所

toilet

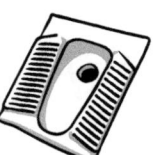

蹲便器

squat toilet

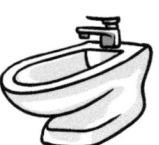

坐浴器

bidet

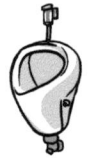

小便斗

urinal

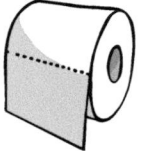

廁紙

toilet paper

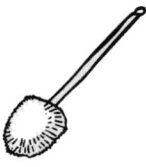

馬桶刷

toilet brush

牙刷
toothbrush

牙膏
toothpaste

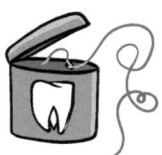

牙線
dental floss

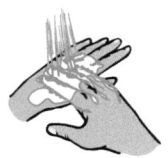

洗
wash

手持式蓮蓬頭
hand shower

沖洗器
douche

洗臉盆
basin

洗背刷
back brush

肥皂
soap

沐浴露
shower gel

洗髮乳
shampoo

法蘭絨
flannel

排水
drain

乳霜
creme

除臭劑
deodorant

浴室 - bathroom

鏡子

mirror

手鏡

hand mirror

刮鬚刀

razor

刮鬚泡沫

shaving foam

鬚後水

aftershave

梳子

comb

刷子

brush

吹風機

hair-dryer

噴髮定型劑

hairspray

化妝品

makeup

唇膏

lipstick

指甲油

nail varnish

化妝棉

cotton wool

指甲剪

nail scissors

香水

perfume

洗漱包

washbag

凳子

stool

計重秤

weighing scales

浴袍

bathrobe

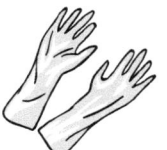

橡膠手套

rubber gloves

衛生棉條

tampon

衛生棉

sanitary towel

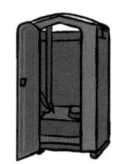

化學廁所

chemical toilet

兒童房

kids room

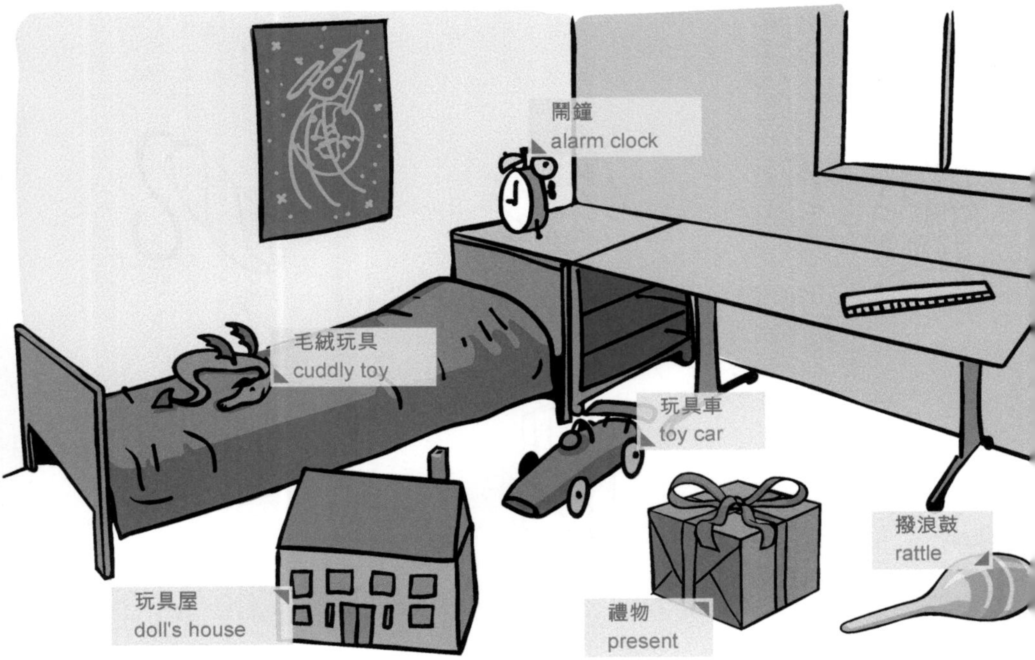

鬧鐘
alarm clock
毛絨玩具
cuddly toy
玩具車
toy car
撥浪鼓
rattle
玩具屋
doll's house
禮物
present

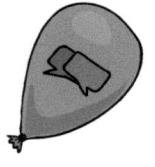

氣球

balloon

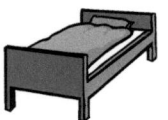

床

bed

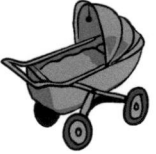

嬰兒車

stroller

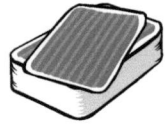

撲克牌

deck of cards

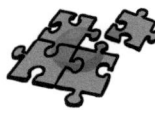

拼圖

jigsaw

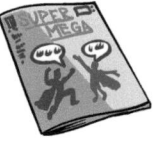

漫畫

comic

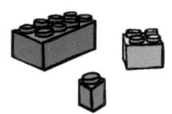

樂高積木

lego bricks

積木玩具

toy blocks

公仔

action figure

嬰兒服

romper suit

飛盤

frisbee

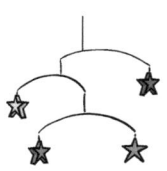

床鈴玩具

mobile

棋盤遊戲

board game

骰子

dice

火車模型

model train set

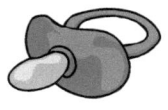

安撫奶嘴

pacifier

派對

party

繪本

picture book

球

ball

洋娃娃

doll

玩

play

沙坑

sandpit

鞦韆

swing

玩具

toys

電玩遊戲

video game console

三輪車

tricycle

泰迪熊

teddy bear

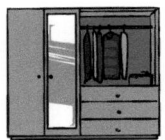

衣櫃

wardrobe

衣服

clothing

襪子

socks

長襪

stockings

緊身褲

tights

圍巾
scarf

雨傘
umbrella

皮帶
belt

T恤
t-shirt

靴子
boots

拖鞋
slippers

運動鞋
sneakers

涼鞋
sandals

鞋
shoes

雨靴
rubber boots

內褲
underwear

胸罩
bra

背心
undershirt

衣服 - clothing

45

身體

body

褲子

pants

牛仔褲

jeans

短裙

skirt

女式襯衫

blouse

襯衫

shirt

套頭衫

pullover

連帽上衣

sweater

西裝夾克

blazer

夾克

jacket

外套

coat

雨衣

raincoat

套裝

costume

連衣裙

dress

婚紗

wedding dress

西裝

suit

睡袍

nightgown

睡衣

pajamas

莎麗

sari

頭巾

headscarf

包頭巾

turban

波卡

burka

卡夫坦

kaftan

(阿拉伯式)長袍

abaya

泳衣

swimsuit

男式泳褲

trunks

短褲

shorts

運動服

tracksuit

圍裙

apron

手套

gloves

鈕扣

button

眼鏡

glasses

手鏈

bracelet

項鍊

necklace

戒指

ring

耳環

earring

便帽

cap

衣架

coat hanger

帽子

hat

領帶

tie

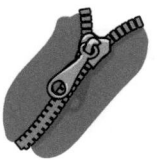

拉鍊

zip

安全帽

helmet

背帶

braces

校服

school uniform

制服

uniform

衣服 - clothing

圍兜
bib

安撫奶嘴
pacifier

尿布
diaper

辦公室
office

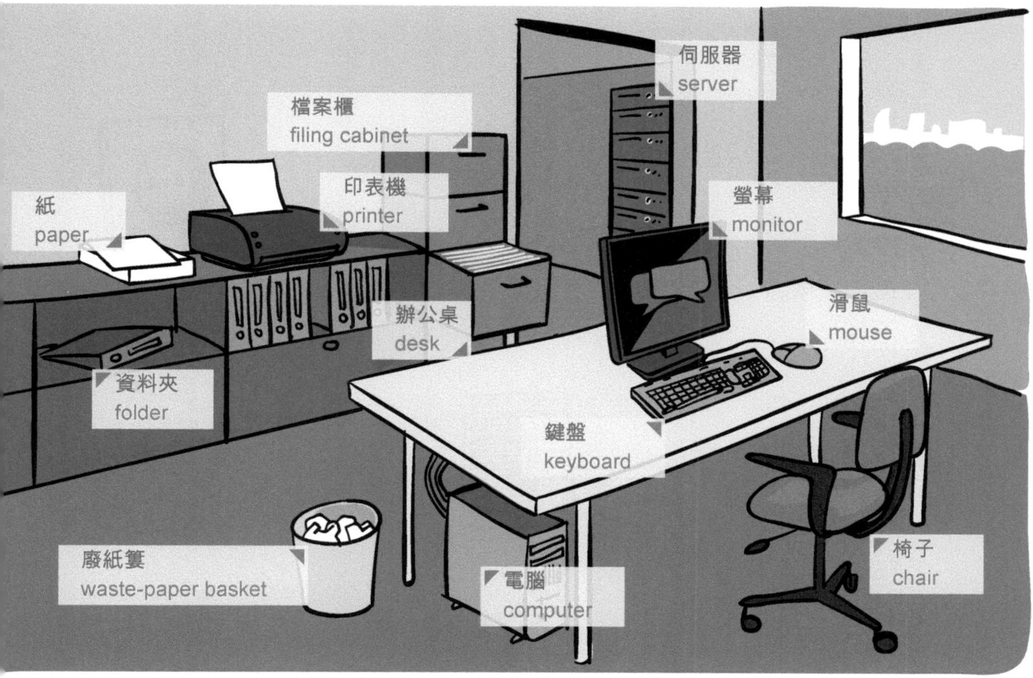

伺服器
server

檔案櫃
filing cabinet

印表機
printer

螢幕
monitor

紙
paper

辦公桌
desk

滑鼠
mouse

資料夾
folder

鍵盤
keyboard

廢紙簍
waste-paper basket

電腦
computer

椅子
chair

咖啡杯
coffee mug

計算機
calculator

網際網路
internet

筆記型電腦
laptop

信件
letter

簡訊
message

行動電話
cell phone

網路
network

影印機
photocopier

軟體
software

電話
telephone

插座
plug socket

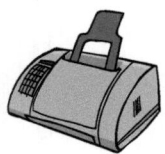

傳真機
fax machine

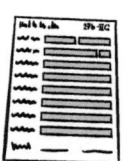

表格
form

檔案
document

買
buy

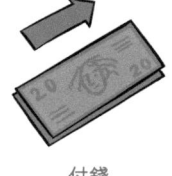

付錢
pay

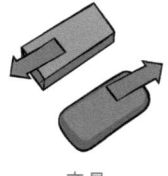

交易
trade

現金
money

美元
dollar

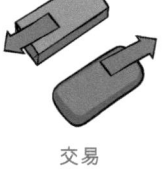 

歐元
euro

日元
yen

盧布
rouble

瑞士法郎
Swiss franc

人民幣
renminbi yuan

盧比
rupee

提款處
cash point

外幣兌換處

currency exchange office

金

gold

銀

silver

石油

oil

能源

energy

價格

price

合約

contract

稅金

tax

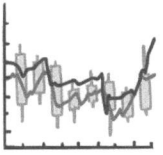

股票

stock

工作

work

職員

employee

老闆

employer

工廠

factory

商店

shop

職業
occupations

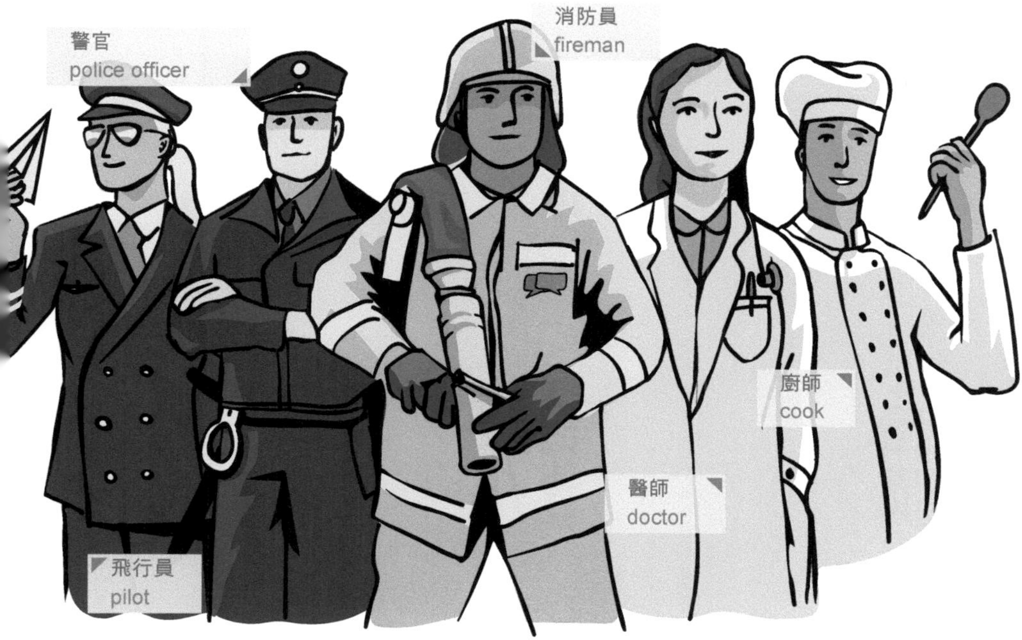
警官
police officer
消防員
fireman
廚師
cook
醫師
doctor
飛行員
pilot

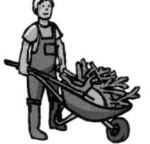

園丁

gardener

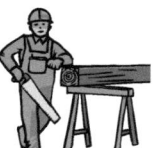

木匠

carpenter

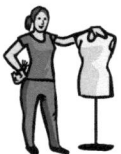

裁縫

seamstress

法官

judge

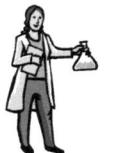

化學家

chemist

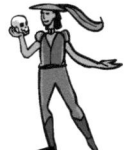

演員

actor

公車司機

bus driver

計程車司機

taxi driver

漁夫

fisherman

清洗女工

cleaning lady

屋頂工

roofer

服務生

waiter

獵人

hunter

畫家

painter

麵包師

baker

電工

electrician

建築工人

builder

工程師

engineer

屠夫

butcher

水管工

plumber

郵差

postman

士兵

soldier

建築師

architect

收銀員

cashier

花農

florist

理髮師

hairdresser

售票員

conductor

機械技師

mechanic

船長

captain

牙醫

dentist

科學家

scientist

拉比

rabbi

伊瑪目

imam

和尚

monk

牧師

pastor

工具

tools

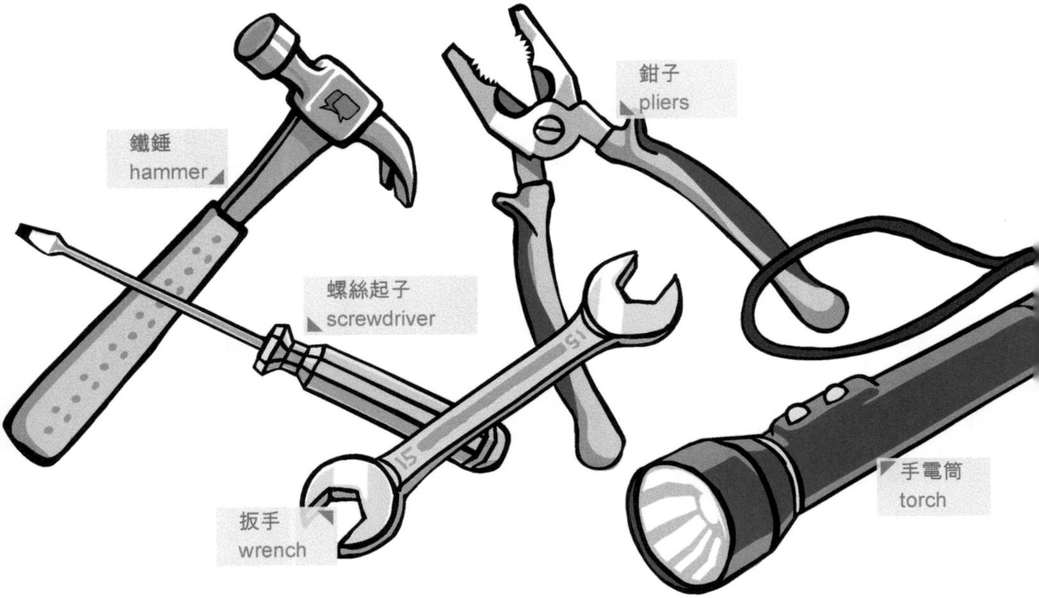

鉗子
pliers
鐵錘
hammer
螺絲起子
screwdriver
扳手
wrench
手電筒
torch

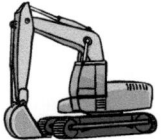

挖掘機

excavator

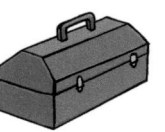

工具箱

toolbox

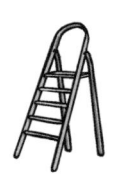

梯子

ladder

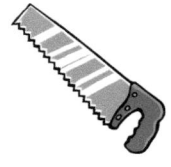

鋸子

saw

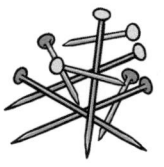

釘子

nails

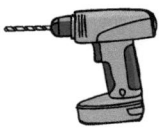

鑽機

drill

修
repair

鏟子
shovel

糟糕！
Damn!

畚箕
dustpan

油漆桶
paint can

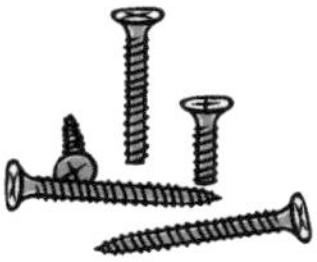

螺絲
screws

樂器
musical instruments

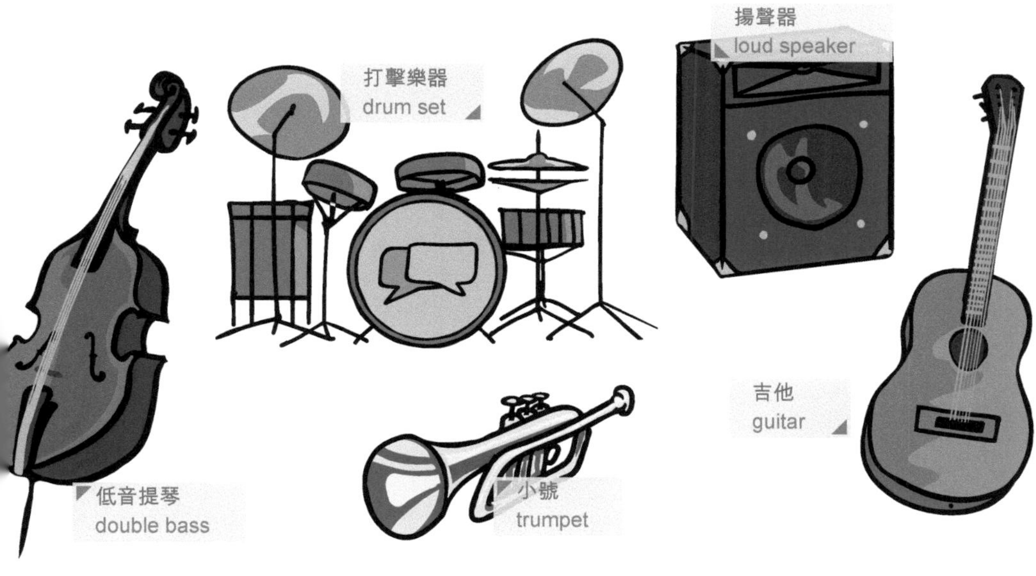

揚聲器
loud speaker

打擊樂器
drum set

吉他
guitar

低音提琴
double bass

小號
trumpet

鋼琴

piano

小提琴

violin

貝斯

bass

定音鼓

timpani

鼓

drums

電子琴

keyboard

薩克斯風

saxophone

長笛

flute

麥克風

microphone

動物園

ZOO

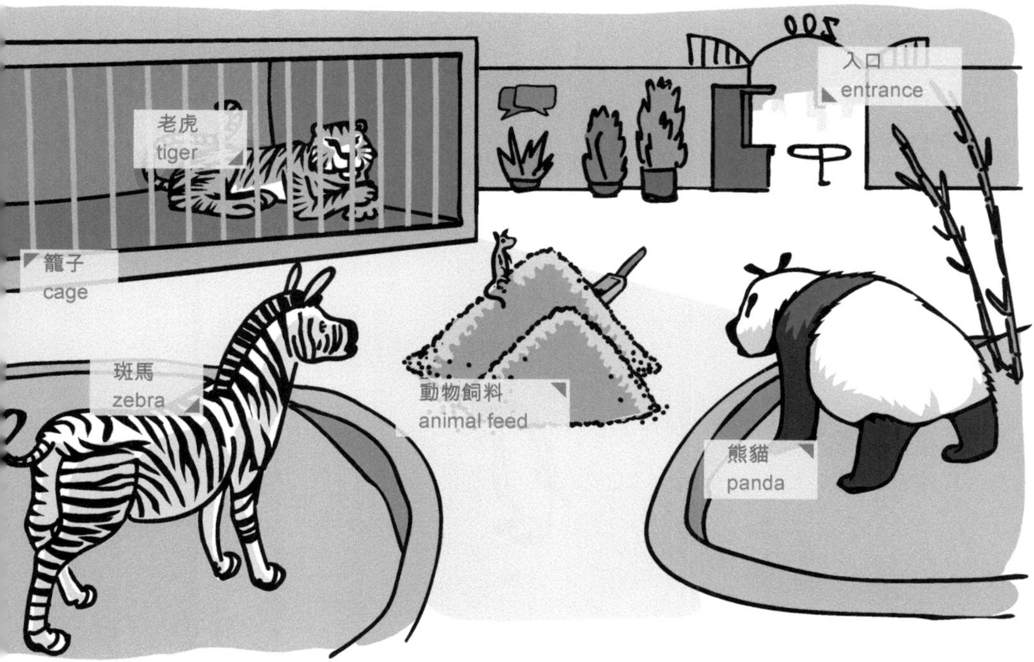

老虎
tiger
入口
entrance
籠子
cage
斑馬
zebra
動物飼料
animal feed
熊貓
panda

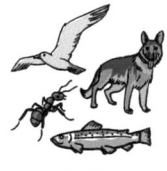

動物
animals

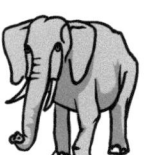

大象
elephant

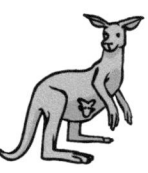

袋鼠
kangaroo

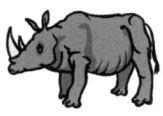

犀牛
rhino

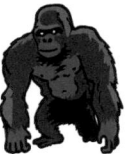

大猩猩
gorilla

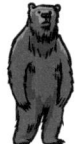

熊
bear

駱駝

camel

鴕鳥

ostrich

獅子

lion

猴子

monkey

紅鶴

flamingo

鸚鵡

parrot

北極熊

polar bear

企鵝

penguin

鯊魚

shark

孔雀

peacock

蛇

snake

鱷魚

crocodile

動物園管理員

zookeeper

海豹

seal

美洲豹

jaguar

矮種馬

pony

豹

leopard

河馬

hippo

長頸鹿

giraffe

老鷹

eagle

野豬

boar

魚

fish

龜

turtle

海象

walrus

狐狸

fox

羚羊

gazelle

橫欖球
American football

騎腳踏車
cycling

網球
tennis

籃球
basketball

游泳
swimming

拳擊
boxing

冰球
ice hockey

美式足球
soccer

羽毛球
badminton

田徑
athletics

手球
handball

滑雪
skiing

馬球
polo

活動
activities

笑
laugh
跳
jump
擁抱
hug
走路
walk
唱
sing
做夢
dream
祈禱
pray
親吻
kiss

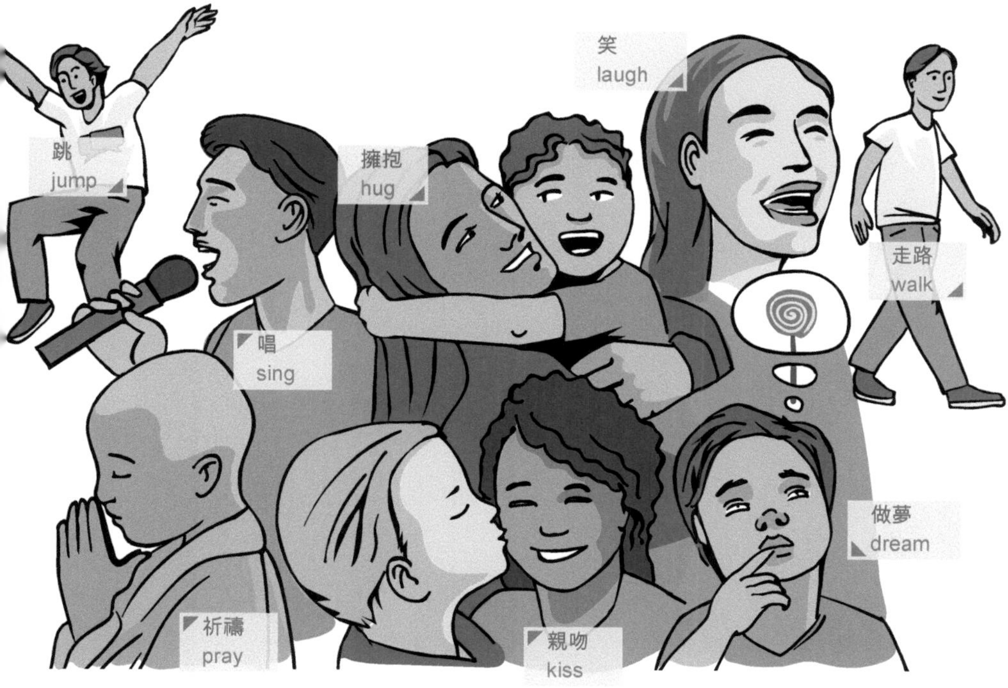

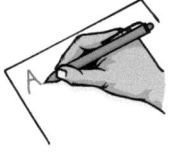

書寫

write

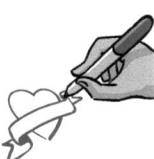

畫

draw

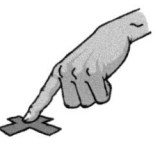

展示

show

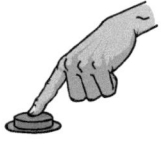

推

push

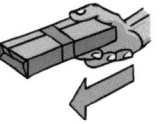

給

give

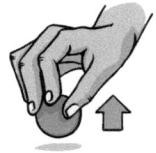

拿

take

有
have

做
do

當
be

站
stand

跑
run

拉
pull

丟
throw

摔倒
fall

躺
lie

等待
wait

攜帶
carry

坐
sit

穿衣
get dressed

睡覺
sleep

醒來
wake up

看
look at

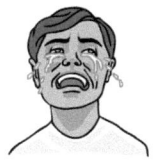

哭
cry

擊
stroke

梳頭
comb

交談
talk

明白
understand

問
ask

聽
listen

喝
drink

吃
eat

清理
tidy up

愛
love

做飯
cook

開車
drive

飛
fly

活動 - activities

航行

sail

計算

calculate

讀

read

學習

learn

工作

work

結婚

marry

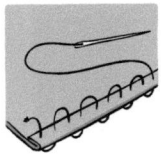

縫

sew

刷牙

brush teeth

殺

kill

抽菸

smoke

寄

send

祖母
grandmother

祖父
grandfather

父親
father

母親
mother

嬰兒
baby

女兒
daughter

兒子
son

客人
guest

阿姨
aunt

叔叔
uncle

兄弟
brother

姐妹
sister

身體

body

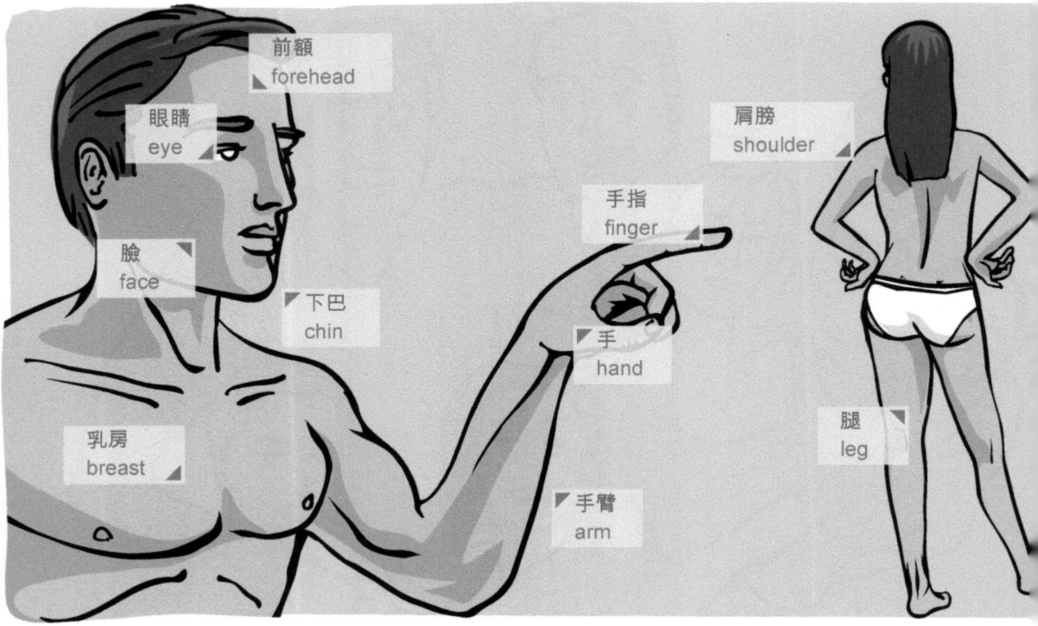
前額
forehead
眼睛
eye
肩膀
shoulder
手指
finger
臉
face
下巴
chin
手
hand
腿
leg
乳房
breast
手臂
arm

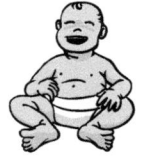

嬰兒

baby

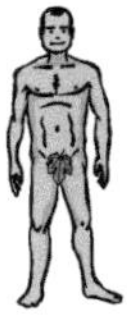

男人

man

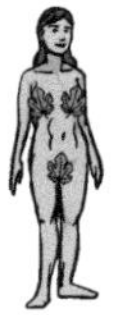

女人

woman

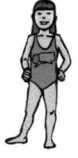

女孩

girl

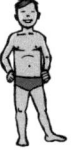

男孩

boy

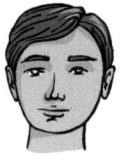

頭

head

背部
back

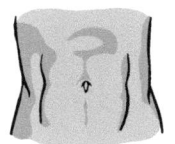
肚子
belly

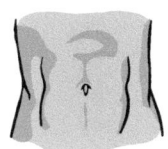
肚臍
navel

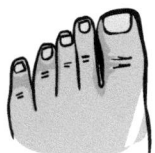
腳趾
toe

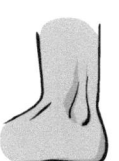
腳後跟
heel

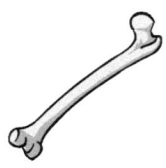
骨頭
bone

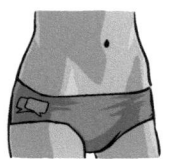
臀部
hip

膝蓋
knee

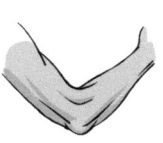
手肘
elbow

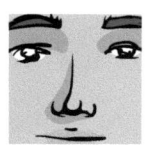
鼻子
nose

屁股
buttocks

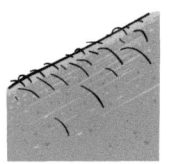
皮膚
skin

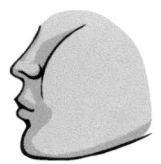
臉頰
cheek

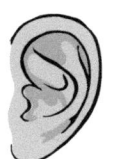
耳朵
ear

嘴唇
lip

身體 - body

嘴
mouth

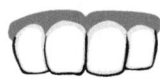

牙齒
tooth

舌頭
tongue

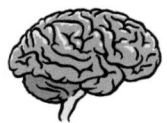

腦
brain

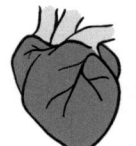

心臟
heart

肌肉
muscle

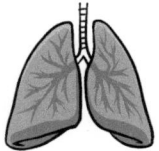

肺
lung

肝臟
liver

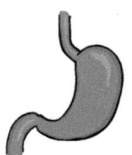

胃
stomach

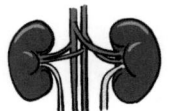

腎臟
kidneys

性交
sex

保險套
condom

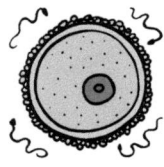

卵子
ovum

精子
semen

懷孕
pregnancy

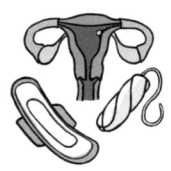

月事

menstruation

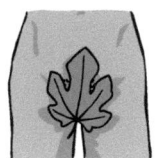

陰道

vagina

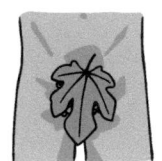

陰莖

penis

眉毛

eyebrow

頭髮

hair

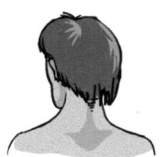

脖子

neck

醫院

hospital

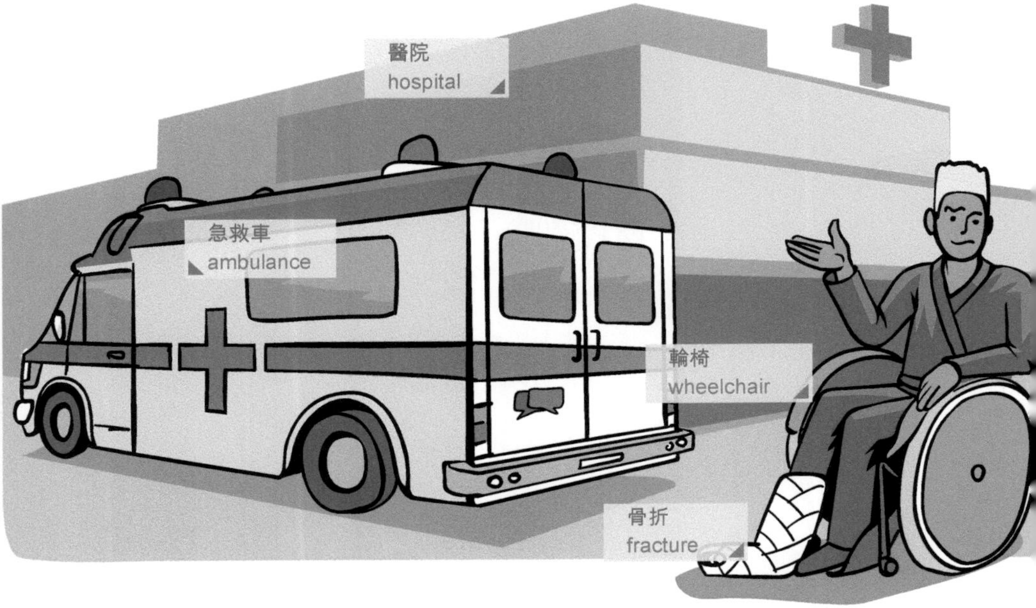

醫院
hospital
急救車
ambulance
輪椅
wheelchair
骨折
fracture

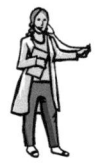

醫師

doctor

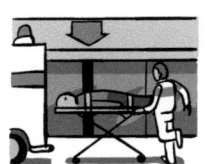

急診室

emergency room

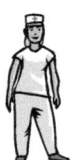

護理師

nurse

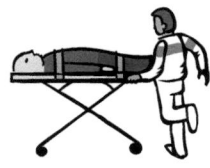

緊急情形

emergency

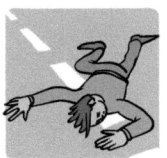

昏迷

unconscious

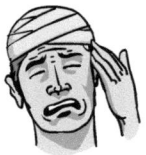

痛

pain

受傷

injury

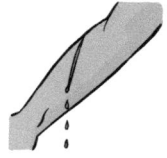

出血

bleeding

心臟病發作

heart attack

中風

stroke

過敏

allergy

咳嗽

cough

發燒

fever

流感

flu

腹瀉

diarrhea

頭痛

headache

癌症

cancer

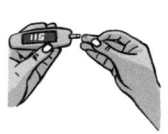

糖尿病

diabetes

外科醫師

surgeon

手術刀

scalpel

手術

operation

電腦斷層掃描
CT

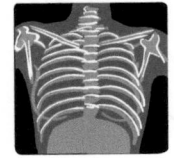

X光
x-ray

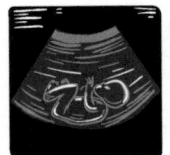

超音波
ultrasound

口罩
face mask

疾病
disease

候診室
waiting room

拐杖
crutch

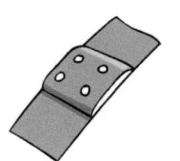

石膏
plaster

繃帶
bandage

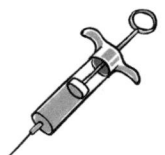

注射
injection

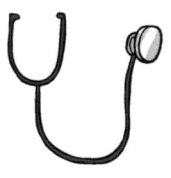

聽診器
stethoscope

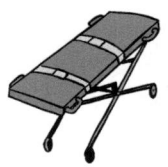

擔架
stretcher

體溫計
clinical thermometer

出生
birth

超重
overweight

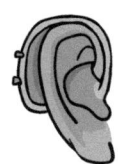

助聽器

hearing aid

消毒液

disinfectant

感染

infection

病毒

virus

愛滋病

HIV / AIDS

藥物

medicine

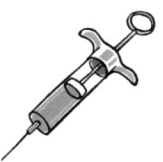

接種疫苗

vaccination

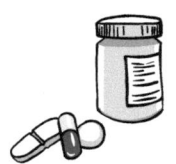

藥片

tablets

藥丸

pill

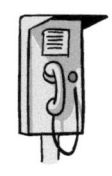

急救電話

emergency call

血壓計

blood pressure monitor

生病/健康

ill / healthy

救命！

Help!

警報

alarm

突擊

assault

攻擊

attack

危險

danger

緊急出口

emergency exit

失火了！

Fire!

滅火器

fire extinguisher

意外

accident

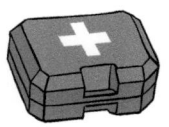

急救箱

first-aid kit

呼救訊號

SOS

員警

police

歐洲

Europe

北美洲

North America

南美洲

South America

非洲

Africa

亞洲

Asia

澳洲

Australia

大西洋

Atlantic

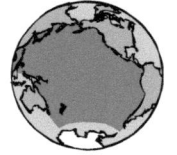

太平洋

Pacific

印度洋

Indian Ocean

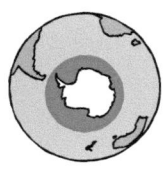

南冰洋

Antarctic Ocean

北冰洋

Arctic Ocean

北極

North pole

南極

South pole

南極洲

Antarctica

地球

earth

陸地

land

海

sea

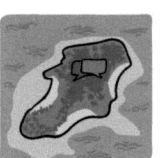

島

island

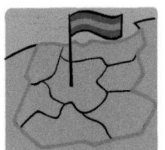

國家

nation

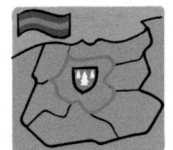

州

state

錶盤
clock face

時針
hour hand

分針
minute hand

秒針
second hand

現在幾點？
What time is it?

天
day

時間
time

現在
now

電子錶
digital watch

分
minute

時
hour

週

week

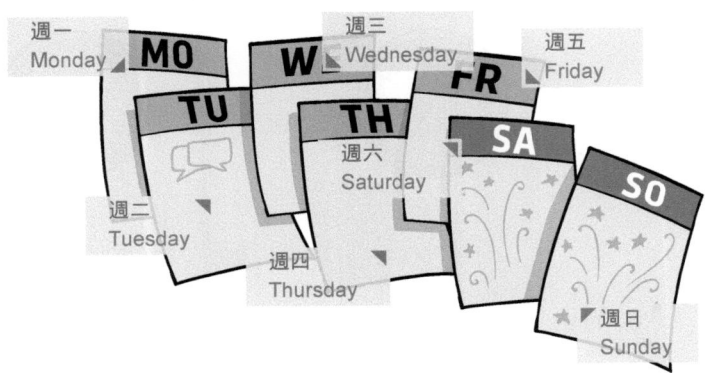

週一 Monday
週二 Tuesday
週三 Wednesday
週四 Thursday
週五 Friday
週六 Saturday
週日 Sunday

昨天

yesterday

今天

today

明天

tomorrow

早晨

morning

中午

noon

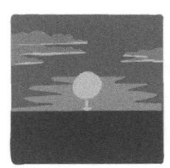

晚上

evening

工作日

workdays

週末

weekend

年

year

雨
rain
彩虹
rainbow
風
wind
雪
snow
春
spring
夏
summer
秋
fall
冬
winter

4.APRIL 11°
5.APRIL 4°
6.APRIL 13°
7.APRIL 8°
8.APRIL 10°

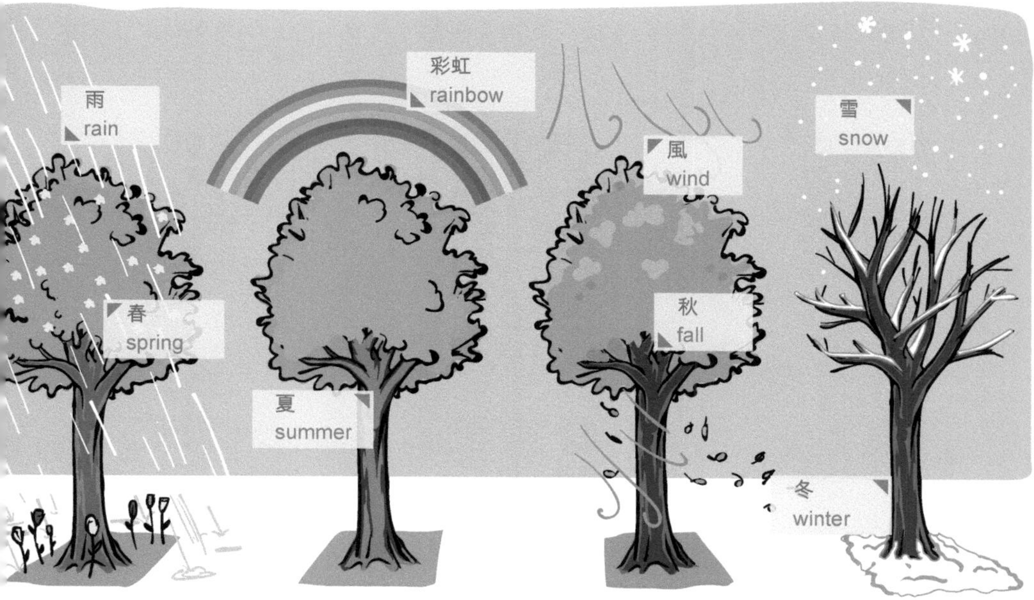

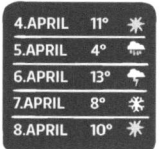

天氣預告

weather forecast

F
C
120
90
60
30
0
-30
40
30
20
10
0
-10
-20

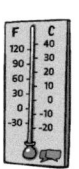

溫度計

thermometer

陽光

sunshine

雲

cloud

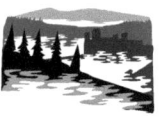

霧

fog

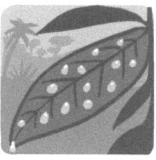

潮濕

humidity

閃電

lightning

打雷

thunder

風暴

storm

冰雹

hail

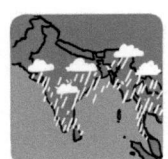

季風

monsoon

洪水

flood

冰

ice

一月

January

二月

February

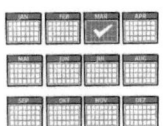

三月

March

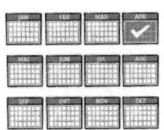

四月

April

五月

May

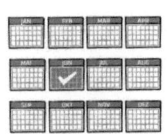

六月

June

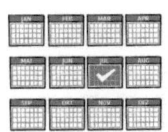

七月

July

八月

August

年 - year

九月

September

十月

October

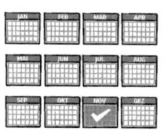

十一月

November

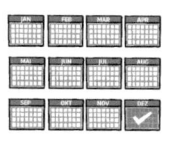

十二月

December

形狀

shapes

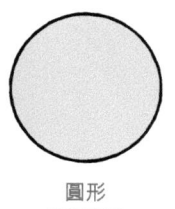

圓形

circle

正方形

square

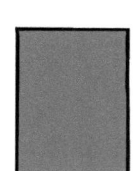

長方形

rectangle

三角形

triangle

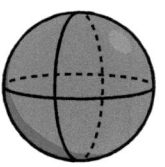

球體

sphere

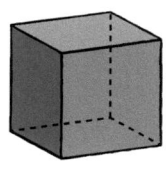

立方體

cube

白
....
white

黃
....
yellow

橙
....
orange

粉
....
pink

紅
....
red

紫
....
purple

藍
....
blue

綠
....
green

棕
....
brown

灰
....
gray

黑
....
black

很多/少許

a lot / a little

生氣/平靜

angry / calm

美/醜

beautiful / ugly

首/尾

beginning / end

大/小

big / small

明/暗

bright / dark

兄弟/姐妹

brother / sister

乾淨/骯髒

clean / dirty

完整/缺失

complete / incomplete

白天/晚上

day / night

死/生

dead / alive

寬/窄

wide / narrow

可食用/非食用

edible / inedible

邪惡/善良

evil / kind

興奮/無聊

excited / bored

胖/瘦

fat / thin

第一/最後

first / last

朋友/敵人

friend / enemy

滿/空

full / empty

硬/軟

hard / soft

重/輕

heavy / light

餓/渴

hunger / thirst

生病/健康

ill / healthy

非法/合法

illegal / legal

聰明/愚笨

intelligent / stupid

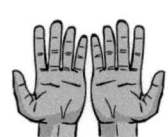

左/右

left / right

近/遠

near / far

新/舊

new / used

沒有/有些

nothing / something

老/幼

old / young

開/關

on / off

打開/闔上

open / closed

安靜/吵鬧

quiet / loud

富/窮

rich / poor

對/錯

right / wrong

粗糙/光滑

rough / smooth

傷心/高興

sad / happy

短/長

short / long

慢/快

slow / fast

濕/乾

wet / dry

溫暖/涼爽

warm / cool

戰爭/和平

war / peace

反義詞 - opposites

0

零
·················
zero

1

一
·················
one

2

二
·················
two

3

三
·················
three

4

四
·················
four

5

五
·················
five

6

六
·················
six

7

七
·················
seven

8

八
·················
eight

9

九
·················
nine

10

十
·················
ten

11

十一
·················
eleven

12

十二
twelve

13

十三
thirteen

14

十四
fourteen

15

十五
fifteen

16

十六
sixteen

17

十七
seventeen

18

十八
eighteen

19

十九
nineteen

20

二十
twenty

100

百
hundred

1.000

千
thousand

1.000.000

百萬
million

英語

English

美式英語

American English

普通話

Chinese Mandarin

印地語

Hindi

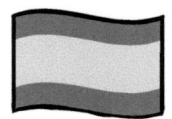

西班牙語

Spanish

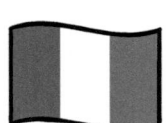

法語

French

阿拉伯語

Arabic

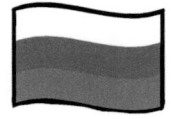

俄語

Russian

葡萄牙語

Portuguese

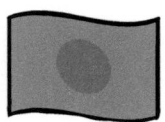

孟加拉語

Bengali

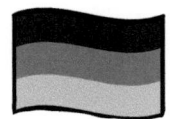

德語

German

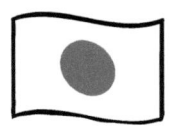

日語

Japanese

我
I

你
you

他/她/它
he / she / it

我們
we

你們
you

他們
they

誰？
who?

什麼？
what?

如何？
how?

何處？
where?

何時？
when?

HELLO, I AM

名字
name

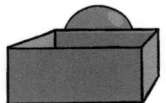

後面

behind

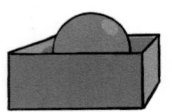

裡面

in

前面

in front of

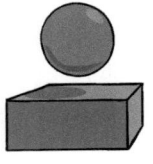

上方

over

上面

on

下麵

under

旁邊

beside

中間

between

地點

place